# Counting to 20
# 4–5

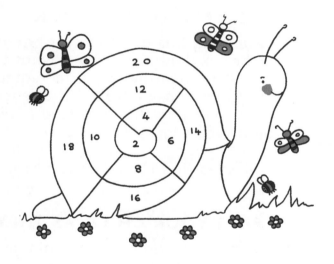

Author: Lynn Huggins-Cooper
Illustrator: Jacqui Bignell

# How to use this book

Look out for these features!

## IN THE ACTIVITIES

The parents' notes at the top of each activity will give you:
► a simple explanation about what your child is learnin
► an idea of how you can work with your child on the activity.

This small page number guides you to the back of the book, where you will find further ideas for help.

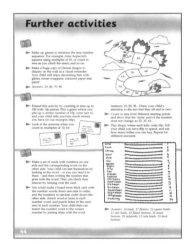

## AT THE BACK OF THE BOOK

Every activity has a section for parents containing:
► further explanations about what the activity teaches
► games that can be easily recreated at home
► questions to ask your child to encourage their learnin
► tips on varying the activity if it seems too easy or too difficult for your child.

You will also find the answers at the back of the book.

## HELPING YOUR CHILD AS THEY USE THIS BOOK

Why not try starting at the beginning of the book and work through it? Your child should only attempt one activity at a time. Remember, it is best to learn little and often when we are feeling wide awake!

## EQUIPMENT YOUR CHILD WILL NEED

► a pencil for writing
► an eraser for correcting mistakes
► coloured pencils for drawing and colouring in.

You might also like to have ready some spare paper and some collections of objects (for instance, small toys, Lego bricks, buttons...) for some of the activities.

# Contents

# Count to 20

Look at these numbers. Say them aloud as you point to each number.

▶ Use the number line to familiarise your child with the numbers 1–20.

▶ Ask them to point to or place counters on different numbers as you say them randomly.

Parents

42

5

# Little Red Riding Hood

Help Little Red Riding Hood to get home safely through the woods. Take turns to roll a die. Move that number of spaces each time, by counting on.

▷ This game will help your child to count up to 20 and back.
▷ Help them to count on each time, for example, from 4 throw a 3. Count '3 more – 5, 6, 7'.

Parents

42

0

11

12

13

14

15

16

17

18

19

20

Now play it backwards so Little Red Riding Hood can follow the path back to 0.

# Looking at big numbers

Look at these large numbers. They are all found in real life. Can you find some large numbers of your own?

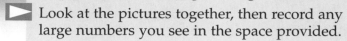

► Looking at numbers in the environment will help your child to recognise large numbers.

► Look at the pictures together, then record any large numbers you see in the space provided.

## My number collection

# How many?

Count the sweets in the sweet shop.
How many can you find?

How many humbugs?

How many lollies?

How many toffees?

How many bags of crisps?

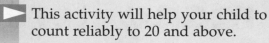

This activity will help your child to count reliably to 20 and above.

Encourage them to write the answers in the boxes.

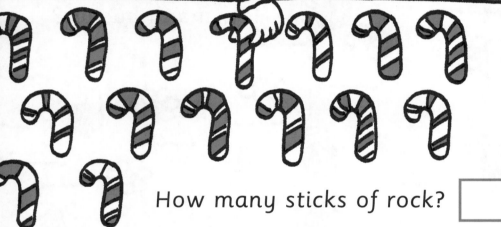

How many sticks of rock?

How many bars of chocolate?

How many cans of pop?

**11**

# How many here?

Count the things you
can see in the park.

How many bushes? ☐

How many flowers? ☐

How many apples? ☐

Parents

This page helps your child to practise counting to 20 and above.

Help them to count all the different things they can see in the picture.

43

How many butterflies?

How many cabbages?

How many carrots?

How many leeks?

How many potatoes?

# Count in twos

Look at this number line. Say it aloud.
Can you say it without looking at it?

| 0 | 2 | 4 | 6 | 8 | 10 | 12 | 14 | 16 | 18 | 20 |

Now look at Sophie Snail.
Point to each shell segment and say the number.
Start in the middle.

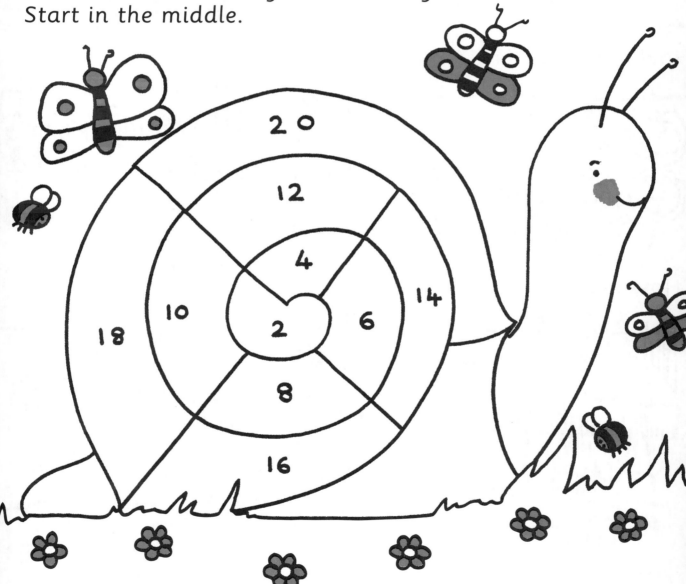

Stanley Snail is missing some numbers on his shell. Write them in for him.

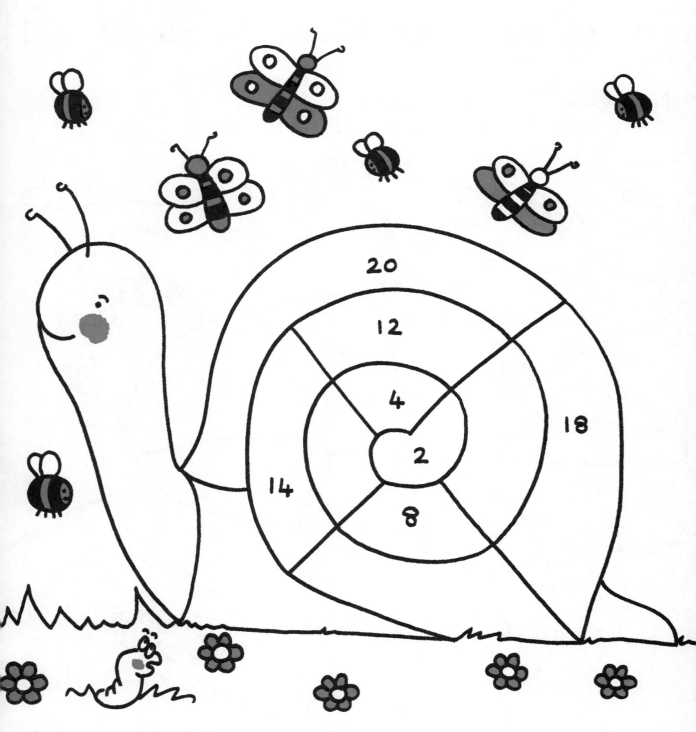

# Count in tens

Look at this number line. Say it aloud.
Can you remember it without looking?

| 0 | 10 | 20 | 30 | 40 | 50 | 60 | 70 | 80 | 90 | 100 |
|---|----|----|----|----|----|----|----|----|----|-----|

Now look at Dennis Dragon
Point to each section and say the number.

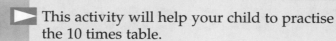

▶ This activity will help your child to practise the 10 times table.

▶ Remind them to use the number line if they get confused.

Parents

44

Davina Dragon is missing some numbers.
Write the numbers in for her.

# Match the envelopes

Draw a line to join the letters to the envelopes with the same numbers.

This activity will help your child to recognise numbers as numerals and words.

Your child should join the number on the stamp with the number word.

# Buttons and beads

Draw a circle around each set of 10 buttons and beads.
How many are left over? How many are there altogether?

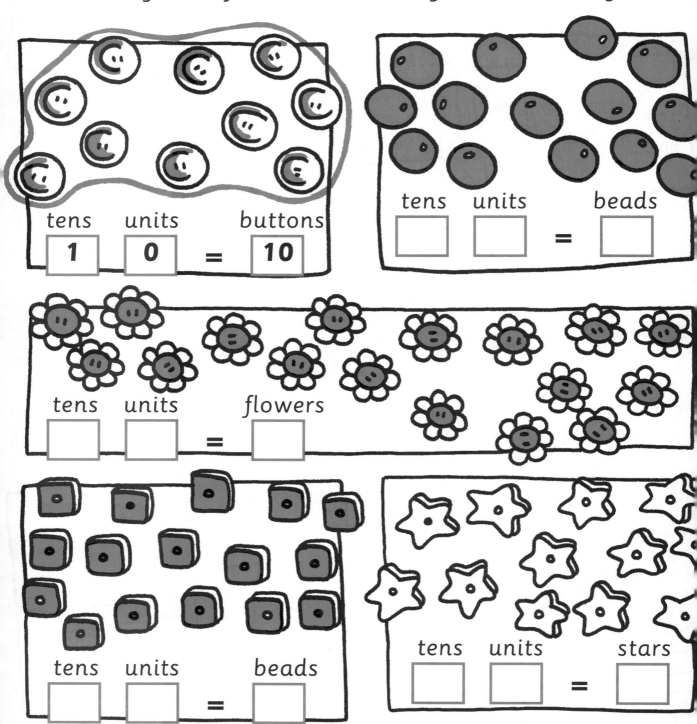

tens    units    buttons

| 1 | 0 | = | 10 |

tens    units    beads

tens    units    flowers

tens    units    beads

tens    units    stars

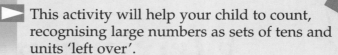
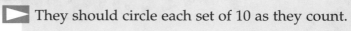

This activity will help your child to count, recognising large numbers as sets of tens and units 'left over'.

They should circle each set of 10 as they count.

Parents

44

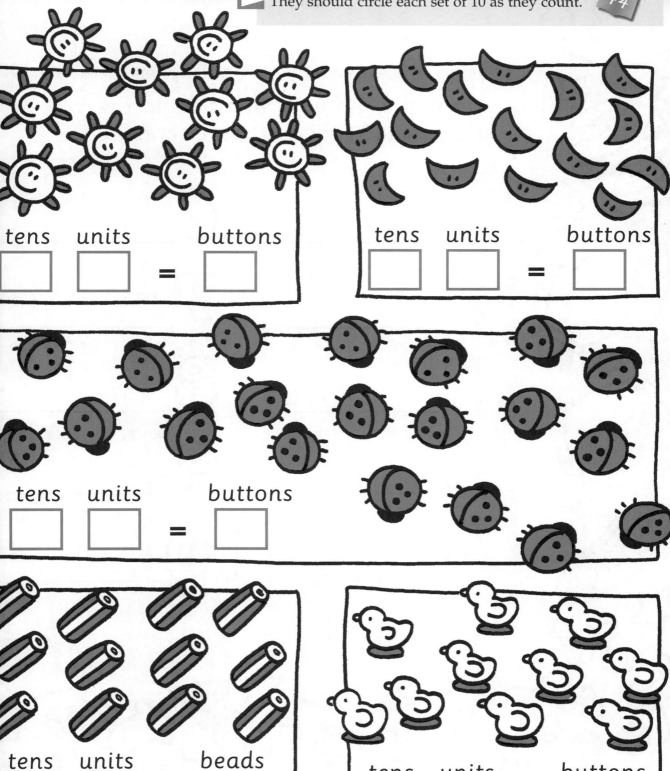

tens    units        buttons

[ ]    [ ]    =    [ ]

tens    units        buttons

[ ]    [ ]    =    [ ]

tens    units        buttons

[ ]    [ ]    =    [ ]

tens    units        beads

[ ]    [ ]    =    [ ]

tens    units        buttons

[ ]    [ ]    =    [ ]

# Writing numbers

Do you write your numbers in the right way? Practise them here.

1 _____

2 _____

3 _____

4 _____

5 _____

6 _____

7 _____

8 _____

9 _____

10 _____

This page helps your child to form numbers correctly. It is an important skill, and mistakes can be hard to correct later!

Your child should trace over the numbers in the directions shown, then practise writing their own numbers.

11 _____    16 _____

12 _____    17 _____

13 _____    18 _____

14 _____    19 _____

15 _____    20 _____

# Which has more?

Look at the bowls of apples. Which do you think holds more? Which holds less? Circle the word you think is correct. Does A have **more/less** than B?

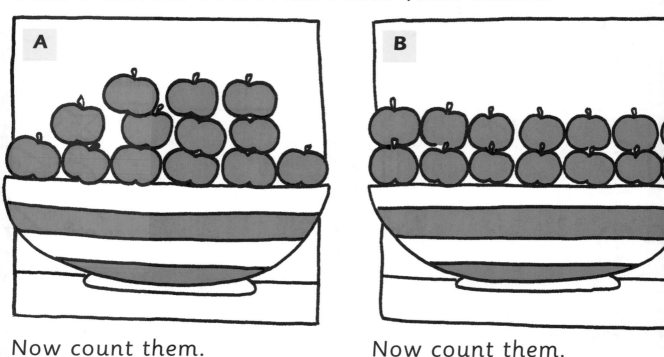

Now count them.

A has [ ] apples

Now count them.

B has [ ] apples

Was your guess correct?
Now circle the larger numbers in each of these.

12 and 20

17 and 12

13 and 17

18 and 8

16 and 11

18 and 19

9 and 12

11 and 16

Parents

This page looks at 'less' and 'more'.

Your child should count the apples and biscuits, and decide which set has more.

45

Now try these.

**A**

A has more/less than B.

**B**

Now count them.

A has ☐ biscuits.

B has ☐ biscuits.

Was your guess correct?

**25**

# Creepy creatures

Fill in the missing numbers.

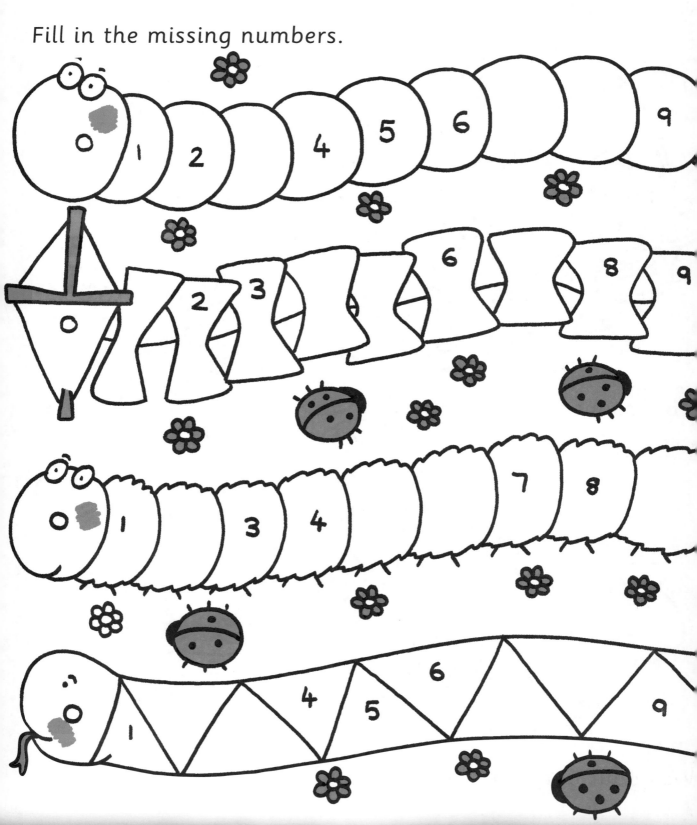

This activity will reinforce your child's recognition of the numbers 1–20.

Count with your child, filling in the missing numbers.

Parents

45

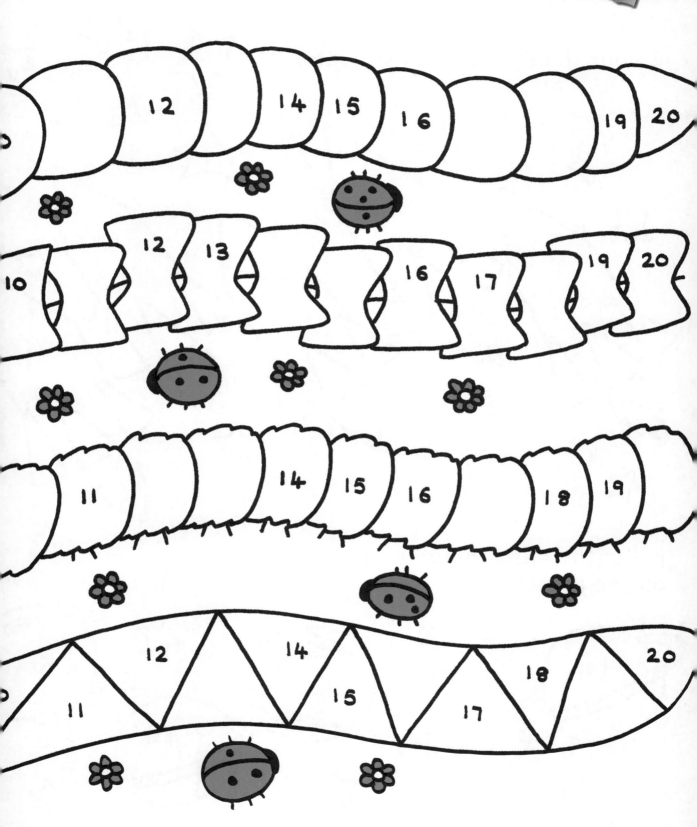

27

# Starship race

Colour the 5th and 9th starship.

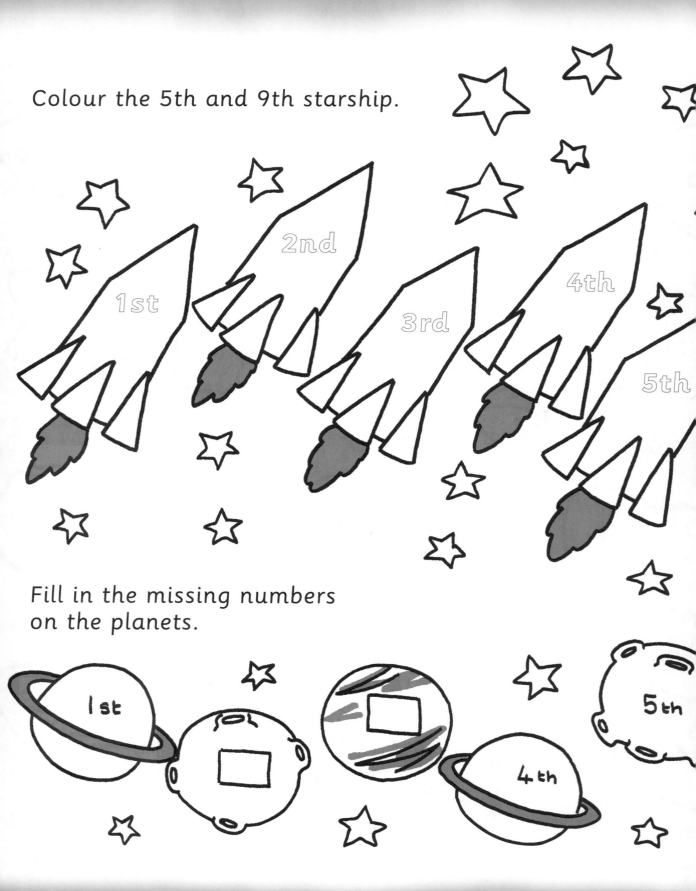

Fill in the missing numbers
on the planets.

This activity introduces ordinal numbers (1st, 2nd, 3rd…). Count along the line of starships with your child.

Say the ordinal numbers aloud as your child works so they link the number to the word.

# Which set has more?

Count the objects. Tick the larger set.

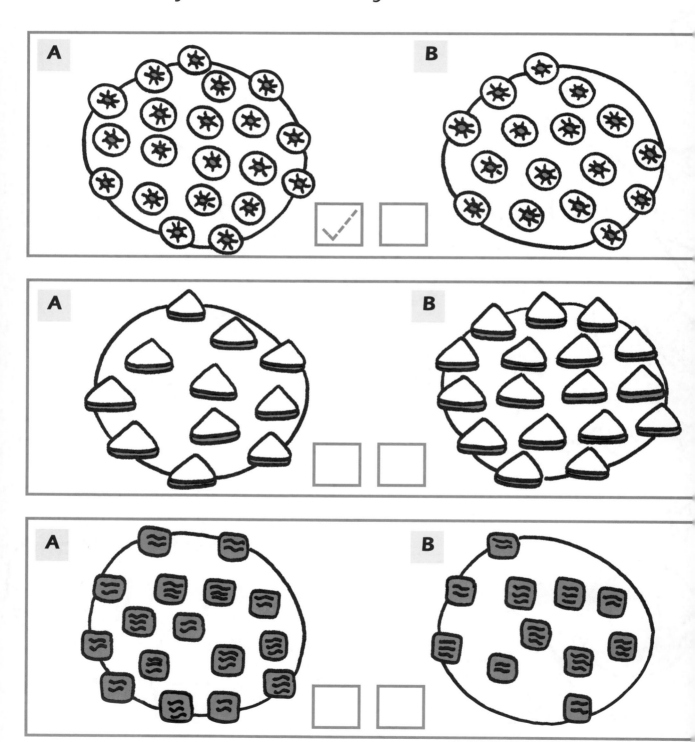

This activity revisits the idea of 'less' and 'more'.

Your child should count the shapes, then tick the larger set.

Parents

46

**A**         **B**

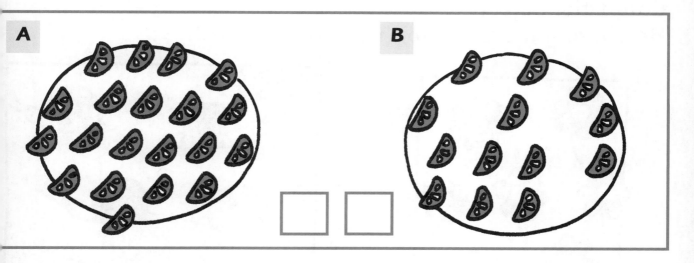

**A**         **B**

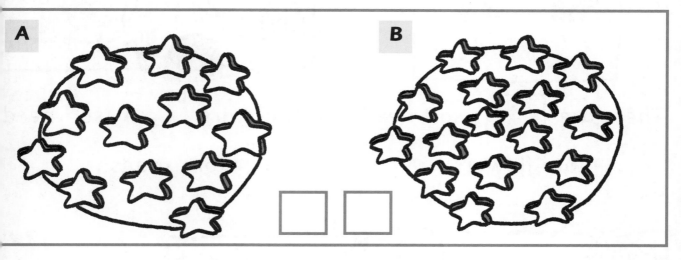

**A**         **B**

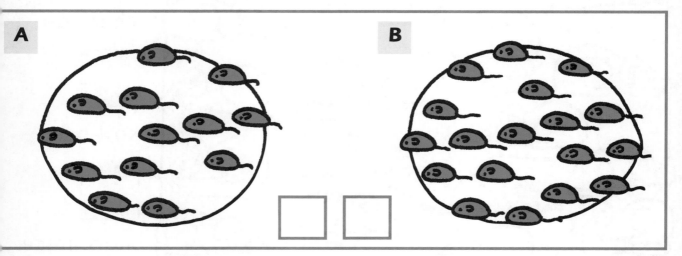

# How many more?

Count the objects.
How many more do you need to make 20?

There are ☐ , so I need ☐ more flowers.

There are ☐ , so I need ☐ more snails.

There are ☐ so I need ☐ more mice.

This activity asks your child to 'count on' from the number of objects to make 20.

Help them to write their answers in the boxes.

There are

so I need

more bananas.

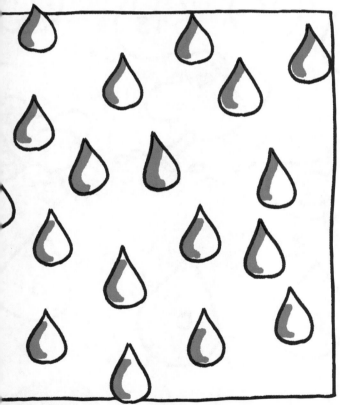

There are [ ] , so I need [ ] more raindrops.

There are [ ] , so I need [ ] more dragonflies.

# Join the numbers

Draw a line to join the pairs of numbers which make 20.

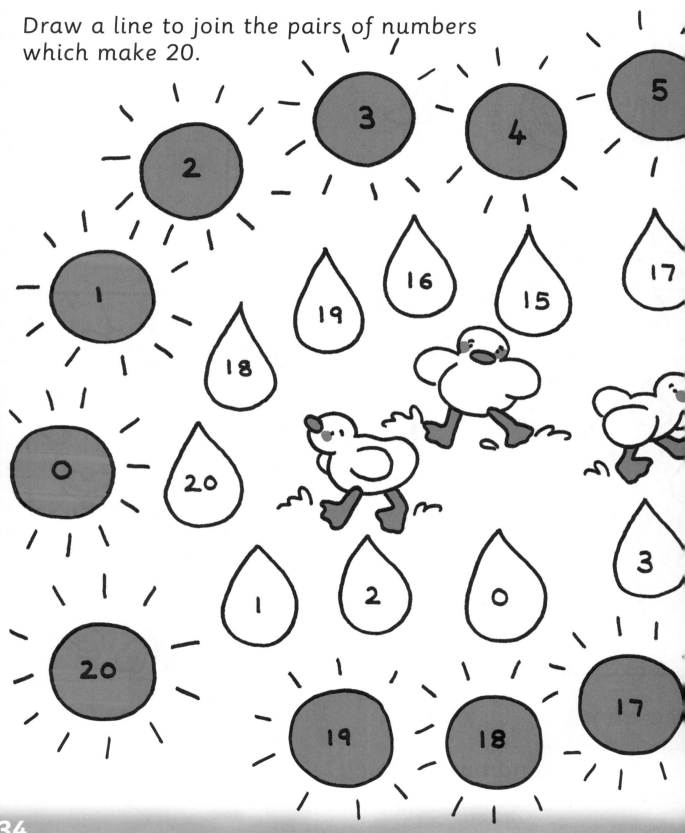

This activity will help your child with calculations and mental arithmetic.

They should draw a line to join the pairs of numbers that make a total of 20.

# What's in the garden?

Count how many objects there are in the garden.

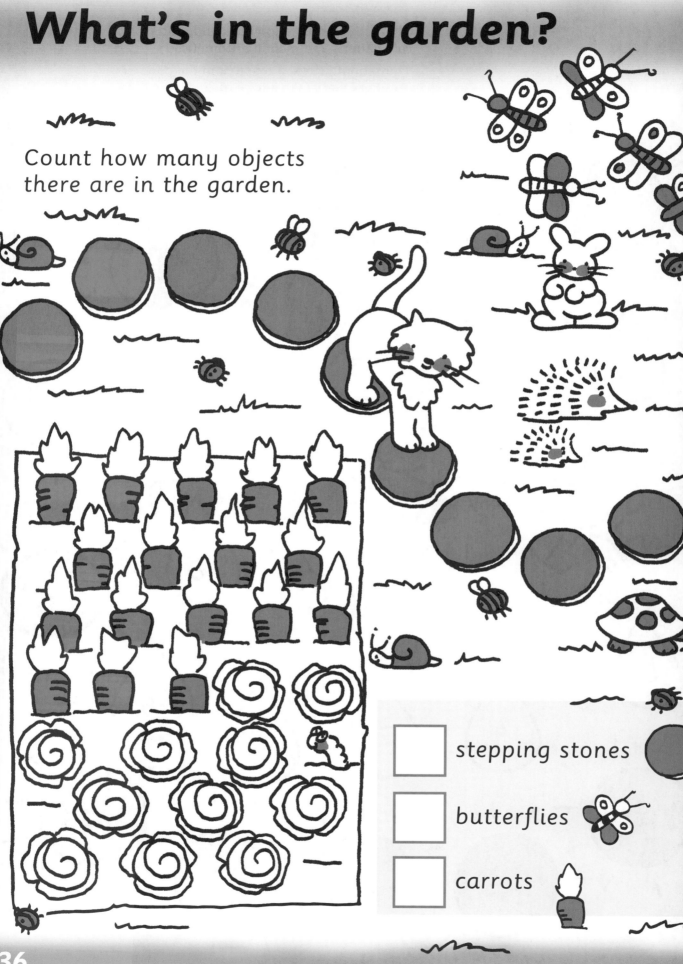

| | stepping stones |
| | butterflies |
| | carrots |

This picture gives your child a chance to practise the counting skills they have learned in this book.

Help them to count the objects without touching each item.

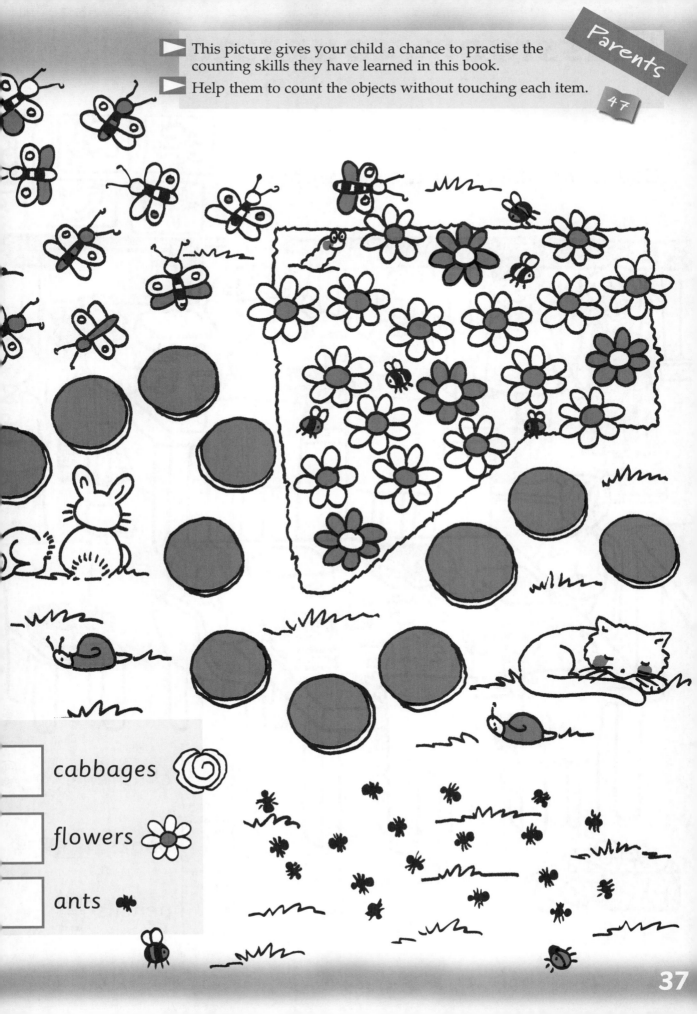

cabbages

flowers

ants

# Classroom counting

Count the objects in the classroom.

| | children |
| --- | --- |
| | books |
| | pencils |

This classroom picture reinforces counting numbers up to 20.

Your child should count the items and write the numbers in the boxes.

47

chairs

lunch boxes

beakers

# Search the park

Count the objects in the park.

| | birds |
| | children |
| | flowers |

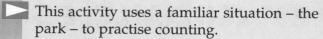
This activity uses a familiar situation – the park – to practise counting.

Your child should count the items and write the numbers in the boxes.

crisps lollies

ice cream drinks sweets

lollies

ladybirds

bubbles

41

# Further activities

 4-5

▶ This activity is designed to familiarise your child with the number sequence from 1–20.

▶ To extend the activity, make a set of cards – perhaps out of cereal packet card. Write the numbers 1–20 on the cards. Lay the cards face down on the floor or table, and ask your child to choose a card. When they look at the card, ask them which number they see.

Ask them questions such as 'Which number comes before…? Which number comes after…? If you count on two more, which number will you have?', and so on.

You can also lay out the numbers in sequence, and remove some cards. Ask your child which cards are missing. Ask them questions such as 'Which number is 2 less than 18? Which number is 3 more than 13?', and so on.

 6-7

▶ Develop the counting activity in a variety of ways. For example, count three numbers in sequence and ask your child to continue. How far can they count? Repeat, but this time down from 20.

▶ Make a habit of counting together as you go about daily life – when you go upstairs and then count backwards as you come down. Take turns when counting to 20, saying alternate numbers with your child.

▶ Play board games such as 'Snakes and Ladders' to practise sequencing numbers.

▶ Make a number line with your child from 0–20 using paper or card. Leave space at the bottom for your child to draw pictures to correspond with the numbers, for instance 1 apple, 2 cats, 3 balls. This will help your child to build a mental picture of what each number represents.

Thread the pieces from a string so you can play games together, such as 'What is the missing number'. (Remember, always be careful when your child plays with string.)

 8-9

▶ This activity is about looking at larger numbers. Ask your child why we have numbers – you may be amazed by their answer!

Ask them what would happen if there were no numbers, for instance, talk about phone numbers – how would we ring Granny/ friends/the doctor if we did not have phone number? How would we know which

S 358 EPk

bus to catch if they did not have numbers?

▶ Make a game of finding numbers, cutting them from newspapers, magazines or timetables. Look for numbers when you are out together – at the shops, on car number plates, Teletext numbers and hymn numbers if you go to a church service.

► You can broaden this activity with plenty of practical experience of counting – at the shops (apples as they go into a bag, sweets in a packet), at home (potatoes in the vegetable rack, chips on the plate, spoons and forks in the drawer, books on the shelf), at the beach ('Can you put 20 stones in this bucket?'), in the woods ('Can you collect 18 leaves?'), in the garden ('Let's pick 13 flowers').

► Encourage your child to count toys as they go back in the cupboard, cars as they come out of the toybox, and so on.

► Make a collection of 'found' natural objects – free and educational! – to help your child to practise counting. Collect shells, pebbles, acorns and pine cones, and keep them in ice cream tubs for this purpose. It is common practice in primary school classrooms. Make a game of asking your child to bring you a given number of things by saying 'Bring me 12 shells'.

► *10–11 answers: 18 humbugs, 17 toffees, 15 lollies, 11 crisp packets, 15 sticks of rock, 12 chocolate bars, 15 cans of pop.*

► *12–13 answers: 11 bushes, 20 flowers, 19 apples, 17 butterflies, 12 cabbages, 16 carrots, 11 leeks, 19 potatoes.*

► There are many ways to practise counting in twos. Look around for things that come in pairs and count them – gloves, socks, shoes, legs on people, ears on dogs, cats or rabbits.

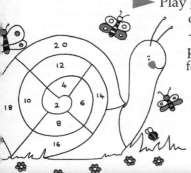

► Play games with counting in twos – it will help to prepare your child for the 2 times table and multiplication.

Ask them how many legs three dolls would have and count them together in twos. Ensure your child does this rather than counting '1 2 3 4 5 6'.

► Teach your child the rhyme '2, 4, 6, 8, who do we appreciate?'. Sing it aloud and accompany it with clapping. Remember, make it fun and they will recall it! Invent some nonsense rhymes for other 'counting in twos' in series, up to 20.

► *Answers: 6, 10, 16.*

# Further activities

▶ Make up games to reinforce the tens number sequence. For example, draw hopscotch squares using multiples of 10, or count in tens as you climb the stairs, and so on.

▶ Make a huge copy of Dennis dragon to display on the wall as a visual reminder. Your child will enjoy decorating him with glitter, sweet wrappers, coloured paper and paint!

▶ *Answers: 20, 40, 70, 90.*

▶ Extend this activity by counting in tens up to 100 with 10p pieces. Play a game where you pile up a certain number of 10p coins (say 6), and your child tells you how much money you have (in our example, 60p).

▶ Look at the answers when you count in multiples of 10, for

instance, 10, 20, 30... Draw your child's attention to the fact that they all end in zero.

▶ Count in tens from different starting points and show that the 'units' part of the number does not change, so 23, 33, 43...

▶ Play shops, where each lolly costs 10p. Tell your child you have 80p to spend, and ask how many lollies you can buy. Repeat for different amounts.

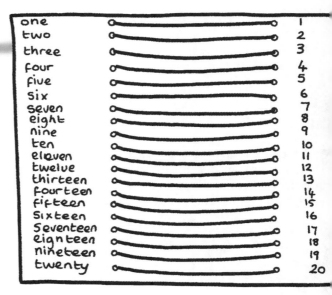

▶ Make a set of cards with numbers on one side and the corresponding word on the other side. Your child can test themselves by looking at the word – or you can read it to them – and then writing the number that goes with the word. They can check their answer by turning over the card.

▶ You could make a board from thick card with the number words down one side in order, and the numbers in random order down the other side. Attach wool or laces to each number word, and punch holes in the card next to each number. Your child then can match the number word to the correct number by joining them with the wool.

▶ *Answers: 14 beads, 17 flowers, 16 square beads, 12 star beads, 10 flower buttons, 16 moon buttons, 20 ladybirds, 12 tube beads, 10 duck buttons.*

▶ Develop this activity by counting out piles of real objects (between 11–20) into sets of ten and what is 'left over'.

This will help your child when they look at 'tens and units' for mathematics. Putting the objects into sets in this way helps your child to 'see' numbers as 'tens and units'.

▶ Broaden this, once your child has had lots of practical experience, by asking 'If we had 13 beads, how many sets of 10 would we have? How many units?'

▶ Repeat this for other numbers from 11–20,

making it fun by saying ridiculous things to make your child laugh. If they have fun, they are more likely to learn and enjoy the activities. You could say things such as, 'If I had 14 spiders in my hat, how many tens would I have? How many units?'

▶ Ask your child to invent some silly numbers for you to work out.

▶ Your child still needs lots of practice forming numbers at this stage, and many children of 4- or 5-years find controlling a pencil quite difficult. Give them lots of encouragement and let them watch you writing numbers. Write them in a large size, with chalk on the pavement or path – perhaps before playing hopscotch!

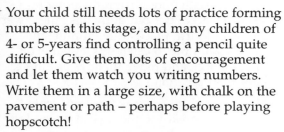

▶ Encourage them to 'finger-write' numbers in the air, and in the sandpit. They would benefit from seeing numbers being written as often as possible, so let them watch as you write lists.

▶ A number line shows the shape of the number, which is important, but does not show the way in which the number is written, so they need as much practical experience as possible.

▶ *Answers: A has less with 13 apples, B has more with 14 apples; larger numbers: 20, 17, 17, 18, 16, 19, 12, 16; A has more with 20 biscuits, B has less with 19 biscuits.*

▶ This activity may be developed by offering lots of practical experience. Give your child piles of objects to count, and ask which has more objects and which has less.

▶ When you look at picture books together, talk about 'more' and 'less'. You can also do this when you discuss toys – animal groups on the farm, vehicles in the garage, and so on.

▶ You could also encourage your child to estimate more and less, and then check their answer with piles of sweets, dried peas or cereal chunks.

*Answers: 3, 7, 8, 11, 13, 17, 18*
*1, 4, 5, 7, 11, 14, 15, 18*
*2, 5, 6, 9, 10, 12, 13, 17, 20*
*2, 3, 7, 8, 13, 16, 19.*

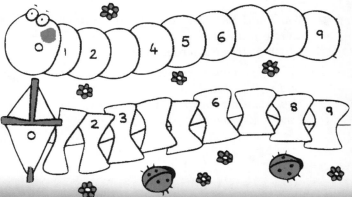

# Further activities

28-29

▶ Write lists of numbers with some missing for your child to fill in.

▶ Count, and take turns to say alternate numbers. Make it fun by adding actions to the numbers, perhaps holding up the number of fingers (and toes!) as you say the numbers.

▶ You could also do the number of jumps as you say the number – you say 'one', and jump once. Your child says 'two', and jumps twice, and so on. By 20 you both will be puffing – but it will help your child to remember the number sequence, and they will want to keep practising!

*Answers: 2nd, 3rd, 6th, 7th, 9th.*

30-31

▶ This activity may be developed by lining up items to practice counting them using ordinal numbers to 'tenth'.

Count with your child, then ask questions such as 'Which car is seventh?'.

▶ Make up a teddy race in the garden. Place the toys in order towards the 'finishing line' and help your child to make up a story about the race and who came where. Your child could pretend to be a TV commentator, and describe the race, with your help…

'And they're off! Teddy is first at the moment, with bunny running along in second place. Poor old dolly has fallen over and is in fourth place at the minute, but there's still time to catch up!' Use lots of imagination, and move the toys around to vary their position.

▶ Help your child to write 'rosettes' from 1st–10th to award to the toys at the end of the race. Make the ceremony fun, and announce the positions as the rosettes are given out.

*Answers: A, B, A, A, B, B.*

32-33

▶ This activity offers your child the opportunity to practise estimating less and more and checking the answer. More practical experience (as described on pages 21–22) would continue to be useful.

▶ You could also carry on offering your child pairs of numbers in order for them to decide which number is larger or smaller.

▶ *Answers: 7 flowers needing 13 more, 8 snails needing 12 more, 16 mice needing 4 more, 11 bananas needing 9 more, 18 raindrops needing 2 more, 12 dragonflies needing 8 more.*

Broaden your child's experience by giving them practical experiences. Give them a variety of objects and ask them how many more they need to make 20.

You could use a range of objects such as natural 'found' materials (cones, shells pasta shapes), dried pulses, sweets, buttons or small toys such as farm animals.

Play a game where you say 'I have a number of buttons (or whatever you choose as your object) hidden under this cloth. It would take 8 more to make 20. How many have I hidden?'

Your child should be encouraged to count on from 8 to 20 to find the answer.

Draw comparisons between number bonds to 10 and number bonds to 20, for instance, 1 + 9 and 11 + 9, 2 + 8 and 12 + 8, 3 + 7 and 13 + 7.

Make the point that the difference is the '1' in front of each number in the second pair. Knowing their number bonds to 10 will help them to learn number bonds to 20.

► *Answers: 20 stepping stones, 15 butterflies, 17 carrots, 11 cabbages, 19 flowers, 18 ants.*

These activities offer your child the chance to practise counting to 20. Other ways you may reinforce this are:

• counting stairs as you climb them

• counting steps as you are walking

• counting collections of items — perhaps making space to display items on a table in groups of 1, 2, 3, 4 to 20 with labels.

Much counting practice can be carried out without preparation during the course of everyday life, for instance, on the beach where you can count 20 pebbles.

When practising with your child, encourage them to count on from a variety of starting points both from 0–20 and from 20–0. Look at the number series together as a pattern.

Looking at numbers from 1–10 and 11–20, can your child recognise a pattern? Can they predict the pattern that will appear when counting from 21–30?

► *38–39 answers: 18 children, 15 books, 18 pencils, 17 chairs, 16 lunchboxes, 18 beakers.*
*40–41 answers: 9 birds, 11 children, 20 flowers, 14 lollies, 15 ladybirds, 18 bubbles.*

# Celebration!

You are so clever!
Colour the stars to show
what you can do!

I can count to 20.

I can count in twos.

I can count in tens.

I know the number words to 10.

I can count from 1st to 10th.